Copyright © 2025 Niranjan Parameshwar

All rights reserved

No part of this book may be reproduced, or stored in a retrieval system, or transmitted in any form or by any means, electronic, mechanical, photocopying, recording, or otherwise, without express written permission of the publisher.

"The ultimate veil that hides reality lies not before our eyes, but behind them: it is the unquestioned certainty that the world is exactly as we perceive it."

NIRANJAN PARAMESHWAR

CONTENTS

Copyright
Epigraph
Preface 3
Introduction: Beyond the Five Senses 5
Part I — Historical and Philosophical Foundations 8
Chapter 1 — The Perennial Mystery 9
Chapter 2 — The Two Worlds 13
Chapter 3 — The Nature of Mind and Cosmos 16
Chapter 4 — Entangled Minds 20
Chapter 5 — Psi in the Laboratory 24
Chapter 6 — Mind Over Matter 28
Part III — Mechanisms and Practices of Expanded Consciousness 32
Chapter 7 — The Unconscious as Bridge 33
Chapter 8 — The Discipline of Mind and Spirit 36
Chapter 9 — The Body as Antenna 41
Part IV — The Future of Consciousness: Neurotechnology, Ethics, and the Great Evolutionary Symphony 45

Chapter 10 — The Connected Brain	46
Chapter 11 — The Ethics of the Open Mind	52
Final Considerations: Toward Unity with Knowledge	56
Bibliography	60

The Hidden Reality of Mind
Telepathy, Synchronicity, and the Future of Consciousness

Niranjan Parameshwar

PREFACE

Since the dawn of civilization, humanity has heard whispers that seem to arise from a realm beyond the senses — intuitions that travel across time and space: the thought that precedes the word, the premonition that comes before the event, the coincidence that repeats until it becomes a message.

These phenomena — telepathy, premonition, synchronicity — endure like invisible threads weaving human experience into the mystery of reality itself.

Rational thought has long tried to confine them to the realm of chance or superstition. Yet, the further science ventures into the depths of consciousness, the more it realizes that the boundary between the subjective and the objective is less a line and more a mirror. The invisible begins to show itself as a legitimate part of the investigation of what is real.

This work is born at that point of convergence. It offers an interdisciplinary journey along the borderlands where philosophy, science, and spiritual tradition meet — regions rarely explored together, yet which, when united, reveal a surprising coherence. Throughout these pages, the Hermetic wisdom of Franz Bardon, the Sufi spirituality of Khawaja Shamsuddin Azeemi, the parapsychological research of Dean Radin, and the ethical reflections of the modern document *Neurotechnology* converse as parts of a single quest: to understand the nature and reach of consciousness.

What the reader will find here is not a manual of beliefs but a map of inquiry. Each chapter was designed to honor the complexity of the subject, avoiding both mystical reductionism and dogmatic skepticism. The purpose is clear: to examine the hidden bridges that unite mind and matter, chance and intention, ancient wisdom and emerging science.

This book is written for those whom Franz Bardon called *"the hungry for knowledge"* — restless spirits who wish to understand, with equal seriousness, both what can be proven and what can only be intuited. It imposes no conclusions but offers conceptual, symbolic, and practical tools so that each reader may craft their own synthesis.

At the end of this journey, one may come to see that reality is not a rigid structure but a sensitive organism that responds to the consciousness observing it — and that the true limit of the human mind is not the mystery itself, but the fear of investigating it.

INTRODUCTION: BEYOND THE FIVE SENSES

The central dilemma of modern consciousness rests on a contradiction that, though disguised by scientific language, continues to challenge human thought.

For classical science, the mind is an epiphenomenon — a fleeting echo produced by the complex machinery of the brain. Yet, ancient traditions, mystics of all ages, and an increasing number of contemporary researchers assert the opposite: that consciousness is not a byproduct but a principle; not the result of matter, but its invisible foundation.

To reexamine this question is not a metaphysical luxury — it is an intellectual necessity. Quantum physics, with its collapse of classical causality, and experimental parapsychology, with over a century of carefully gathered data, demand a radical revision of what we call "reality." Both point to a universe in which mind and matter are not separate entities but complementary expressions of a single field of interconnection.

Common perception, sustained by the five senses, builds for us an illusion of solidity and separation. As Swami Panchadasi observed, the senses are but partial instruments — clouded windows opening onto an infinitely wider horizon. What we take as "objective reality" is largely an adaptive translation: useful for survival, but incapable of revealing the whole of the real.

The "classical world," built upon the pillars of locality and linear causality, has crumbled under the weight of new evidence. In its place rises the "new reality" described by Dean Radin: a nonlocal, entangled universe where thought and event may be linked through channels that transcend space and time. Within this framework, psychic phenomena — once treated as anomalies — begin to appear as natural consequences of an interconnected physical reality.

To explore this new territory of the mind, this book unfolds as a journey in four complementary stages:

Part I — Historical and Philosophical Foundations: tracing the evolution of the study of mind from the oracles of Antiquity to the mystical and cosmological models that shaped human thought.

Part II — The Scientific Evidence for the "Impossible": examining the experiments and discoveries that challenge the materialist paradigm, including studies on telepathy, precognition, and mind–matter interaction.

Part III — Mechanisms and Practices of Expanded Consciousness: analyzing psychological processes and Hermetic or spiritual disciplines that enable the expansion of perception and the conscious mastery of subtle faculties.

Part IV — The Future of Consciousness: exploring the ethical and existential implications of emerging brain technologies, as well as the hypothesis of a collective evolution of human awareness.

To understand where we are heading, we must revisit where we began — the traditions, experiences, and intuitions that dared to affirm that the mind is greater than the brain, and that the invisible is as real as the tangible.

Let us, therefore, follow the thread of this ancient and nearly forgotten investigation — the human journey in search of the hidden reality of the mind.

PART I — HISTORICAL AND PHILOSOPHICAL FOUNDATIONS

CHAPTER 1 — THE PERENNIAL MYSTERY

From Ancient Oracles to Psychic Research

"Every soul is, by its very nature, a seer."
— Plotinus, *Enneads*

The investigation of psychic phenomena is not a modern fad but a continuous thread woven through the entire tapestry of human history.

From the earliest records of civilization, humankind has sensed that there is more to the mind than thought, more to perception than the eyes can see.

What we now call *psychic phenomena* — intuitions, visions, premonitions, subtle communications — once belonged to the domain of oracles, prophets, and sages who served as bridges between the visible and the invisible.

In ancient Mesopotamia, priests interpreted omens in the movements of the stars and the entrails of sacrificed animals.

In Greece, the temple of Delphi stood at the heart of a sacred science, where the unseen spoke through the enigmatic voice of the Pythia.

Plato and Xenophon recount that Socrates possessed a *daimón* — an inner presence that warned and guided him — perhaps the earliest philosophical testimony to intuition as a real and autonomous faculty of the soul.

With the advent of the scientific age, these phenomena did not vanish; they merely changed their language.

The eighteenth century witnessed the rise of mesmerism and the so-called "magnetic somnambulism," which fascinated and divided Europe's academies.

Out of these experiments, the nineteenth century saw the explosion of modern spiritualism — a movement that not only captivated the popular imagination but also inspired rigorously empirical inquiry.

It was in this context that the **Society for Psychical Research (SPR)** was founded in London in 1882 — the formal birth of modern parapsychology.

Composed of eminent Cambridge scholars such as **Henry Sidgwick, Frederic Myers,** and **Edmund Gurney**, the SPR dared to apply the scientific method to phenomena the academic orthodoxy refused even to name.

Its purpose was not proselytism but discernment: to separate the authentic from the illusory, the fact from the fraud.

Even so, the epistemological challenge was immense.

As researcher **Stella Maris Souza Marques** observes, modern science was built upon a program of "systematic distancing from anything that might sound subversive."

Instrumental reason, shaped by the mechanistic paradigm, closed itself off to the imponderable.

The result was a double impoverishment: on one side,

the deeper field of human experience was overrun by charlatanism; on the other, science itself lost the opportunity to widen its horizon.

Henry Sidgwick, writing to a colleague, expressed the frustration of one who saw knowledge bound in an intellectual straitjacket:

"It is a scandal that the debate over the reality of these phenomena still needs to be fought."

Yet the obstacle to accepting the invisible is, above all, philosophical.

The Western mind — heir to Aristotelian and Cartesian thought — was built upon the principle of linear causality: a chain of cause and effect that excludes any form of non-mechanical connection.

However, what ancient traditions and modern psychic experiences share in common is precisely the violation of that logic.

They are united by another, subtler, and more encompassing principle: **synchronicity** — a term Carl Gustav Jung used to describe meaningful coincidences that link external events with inner states of consciousness, without any evident causal relationship.

Synchronicity is the language of the invisible; it is the grammar that connects the oracle of Delphi to the parapsychology laboratory, Socrates' *daimón* to modern telepathic experiments.

Before grasping the implications of this principle, we must acknowledge what history increasingly reveals:
the investigation of the hidden mind is as old as thought itself.

And perhaps the true progress of science lies not in denying mystery, but in learning how to converse with it.

CHAPTER 2 — THE TWO WORLDS

Causality and Synchronicity

"Chance is perhaps the pseudonym of God when He does not wish to sign."
— Anatole France

Causality is the great foundation of Western scientific thought.
According to its principle, every effect must have a preceding cause, and the universe unfolds as an unbroken chain of causes and consequences.
This logical structure — inherited from Aristotle and solidified by Newton — made scientific progress possible, but it also confined reality within a linear, predictable, and self-enclosed model.

In contrast, *Carl Gustav Jung* proposed a complementary principle of connection: *synchronicity*.
He defined it as *"the simultaneous occurrence of two events linked by meaning rather than by cause."*
In other words, synchronicity is the moment when the universe seems to reveal its inner coherence — not through the mechanics of causes, but through the *resonance of meaning*.

Jung illustrated this idea with a now-famous episode from his clinical practice.
He was treating a patient whose rigid rationalism blocked all therapeutic progress.
One day, as she was recounting a dream in which she received a golden scarab, a soft tapping was heard at the window.
Jung opened it and caught a golden-green beetle — a *Cetonia aurata*, the closest European equivalent to the scarab of her dream.
Handing it to her, he said: *"Here is your scarab."*
The symbolic impact was immediate: the "impossible" event shattered her intellectual defenses and opened the path to inner transformation.

In this episode, the link between the dream and the insect is *not causal but archetypal*.
Both are manifestations of the same symbol — the *scarab*, an ancient Egyptian emblem of rebirth and metamorphosis.
It is the *tertium comparationis*, the "third element of comparison" described by Jung: the shared meaning that connects the inner and outer worlds.
Thus, *synchronicity is not a whim of chance, but the eruption of a symbolic order underlying reality.*

Experiments in *Extra-Sensory Perception (ESP)* conducted by *J. B. Rhine* and his successors offered an empirical parallel to this concept.
Physical distance did not diminish the accuracy of responses, and future events seemed to be perceived before they occurred.
Such findings defy the principles of spatial contiguity and temporal succession — the very pillars of classical

causality.

Jung concluded that *"where space and time become relative to the psyche, the concept of cause simply becomes unthinkable."*

This vision finds a deep echo in Eastern philosophy.

Jung related synchronicity to the Chinese notion of the *Tao* — the universal principle that organizes events according to a pattern of meaning rather than a causal sequence.

In Taoist thought, the world is *not a machine but a melody*, where each note manifests precisely when the whole requires it.

What we call "chance" is merely *synchronicity not yet understood.*

Western Hermetic and mystical traditions also recognized this principle, though under different names.

Hermes Trismegistus expressed it in the axiom: *"That which is above is like that which is below."*

It is an archetypal intuition of the interconnection between distinct planes of reality.

Hermeticism understood the universe as woven not by collisions but by *correspondences* — not by impacts, but by *analogies.*

Thus, *causality* describes how the visible world functions, while *synchronicity* reveals the meaning that permeates it.

The first governs the realm of *quantities*; the second, the realm of *qualities.*

Where one measures, the other interprets.

And when both are united, they unveil the deeper architecture of reality:

a living, symbolic cosmos in which mind and world are expressions of a single, silent intelligence.

CHAPTER 3 — THE NATURE OF MIND AND COSMOS

Hermetic and Mystical Models

"That which is above is like that which is below, and that which is below is like that which is above, to accomplish the miracles of one thing."
— *Emerald Tablet of Hermes Trismegistus*

The inquiry into the nature of mind and cosmos has always been the meeting ground — and often the battlefield — of science, philosophy, and mysticism.

Yet the ancient esoteric traditions never perceived a split between *mind* and *matter*; for them, both are expressions of a single primordial substance whose essence transcends all dualism.

This ontological unity forms the foundation of all Hermetic, alchemical, and mystical models, in which the cosmos is not a cold machine but a *living organism endowed with intelligence.*

The Hermetic teachings — particularly as articulated by *Franz Bardon* — describe the universe as the manifestation of four elemental principles: *Fire, Water, Air,* and *Earth*, all

emerging from *Akasha*, the primordial ether.
These are not chemical substances but *universal archetypes*:
Fire symbolizes expansion and electrical energy;
Water, contraction and magnetic force;
Air, harmony and dynamic balance;
and *Earth*, the crystallization of the synthesis of the three.

This cosmology seeks not only to explain the physical universe but also its *subtle planes* — the astral and the mental — establishing a correspondence between *macrocosm and microcosm*.
Within this vision, the human being is a miniature universe; the psychic structure of man mirrors the same laws that govern the stars.

Bardon's "occult anatomy" is thus more than symbolic. It portrays the human being as a *multilayered field of energy*, in which each element operates on a specific level.
The equilibrium between Fire and Water, for instance, determines harmony between *will and emotion, action and receptivity*.
Illness — whether physical or mental — is interpreted as a disturbance of these fundamental principles.
Hence, the process of Hermetic initiation is ultimately the *restoration of cosmic order within the individual self*.

Similarly — though in a more idealistic tone — the *Sufi tradition*, especially as expressed by *Khawaja Shamsuddin Azeemi*, envisions a universe governed by the power of *thought*.
Azeemi conceives thought as the *original substance of creation*, the energetic matrix from which all forms emerge. The physical body, he writes, is merely the *"garment of the soul,"* a temporary interface through which consciousness acts upon the material world.

Communication between minds, according to this view, occurs through *"waves of the Ego"* — subtle vibrations that transcend space and time.
In this model, telepathy and other psychic phenomena are *not exceptions to human nature, but expressions of its original structure.*

If Bardon emphasizes the *architecture* of the universe — the *how* of creation — Azeemi emphasizes its *agency* — the *why*.
Both, however, converge on a single essential insight: *the interconnection of all things.*
The separation between subject and object, between thinker and thought, is an illusion of limited consciousness.
At the deepest level, everything vibrates in resonance within *one reality* whose divisions are only apparent.

Within this framework, the distinction between *conscious* and *unconscious* acquires a new meaning.
The conscious mind, bound to the senses and to discursive reason, is like a lamp illuminating only what lies nearby.
The unconscious, by contrast, is an *ocean where all consciousnesses meet* — the reservoir of cosmic memory.
Through this vast domain, the human soul connects with the astral and mental planes, becoming the vehicle for experiences such as *intuition, clairvoyance,* and *telepathy.*

Curiously, twentieth-century physics — particularly with the rise of *quantum mechanics* — brought forth concepts that echo these ancient mystical models.
Quantum *entanglement* and *indeterminacy* suggest a universe in which separation is illusory, and in which consciousness itself, in some way, participates in the act of observation and the creation of reality.
What was once *symbolic language* now finds its parallels

in mathematics — which, though not explaining the mystery, at least legitimizes it as a plausible philosophical hypothesis.

Ultimately, both Hermeticists and Sufis affirm that *to understand the universe is to understand the mind — and vice versa.*

The mind is the cosmos in miniature; the cosmos, the mind in majestic expansion.

Between them there is no boundary, only gradations of awareness.

The wise man, therefore, does not seek to escape the world but to *recognize it as a mirror of himself.*

"Know thyself, and thou shalt know the universe and the gods."

— Delphic maxim inscribed in the Temple of Apollo at Delphi

Part II — The Scientific Evidence for the "Impossible"

CHAPTER 4 — ENTANGLED MINDS

Quantum Physics and the New Reality

"Those who are not shocked when they first come across quantum theory cannot possibly have understood it."
— *Niels Bohr*

Quantum physics emerged in the twentieth century as an *epistemological rupture without precedent* — a decisive blow to the Newtonian mechanism that had governed scientific thought for more than two centuries.

Its discoveries challenged not only classical physics but also the very foundations of philosophy: our notions of *reality, causality,* and *mind.*

By dismantling the assumptions of separation and objectivity, quantum theory unveiled a profoundly interconnected universe, one in which the observer participates in the very formation of the observed phenomenon.

At the heart of this revolution lies *quantum entanglement* — one of the most astonishing yet rigorously verified discoveries in modern science.

Dean Radin, psychologist and researcher at the Institute

of Noetic Sciences, describes entanglement as *"the deepest discovery in physics,"* not only for its technical implications but for its ontological ones: if everything in the universe was once connected, then *separation is a functional illusion, not an ontological reality.*

Classical physics rested upon five pillars: *objective reality, locality, linear causality, continuity,* and *determinism.*

Each of these has been eroded by quantum experience.

The celebrated *double-slit experiment* of the early twentieth century revealed that subatomic particles such as electrons and photons behave as waves when unobserved, but collapse into particles when measured.

Observation, therefore, is not a passive recording of reality; it is the *creative act* that determines which reality manifests.

The boundary between observer and observed becomes porous — or rather, *nonexistent.*

The *EPR paradox* (Einstein–Podolsky–Rosen), proposed in 1935, was intended to expose this indeterminacy.

Einstein, uneasy with what he saw as the "incompleteness" of quantum theory, called entanglement *spukhafte Fernwirkung* — "spooky action at a distance" — an expression that, ironically, captured the phenomenon perfectly.

Decades later, the experiments of *Alain Aspect*, and subsequently *Anton Zeilinger* and collaborators, confirmed what once seemed absurd: entangled particles truly influence one another instantaneously, violating the principle of locality.

Space, therefore, is *no barrier to communication at the deepest level of nature.*

This discovery reconfigures the entire foundation of

modern ontology.

The universe is not a collection of isolated objects, but an *indivisible web of relations.*

Everything that exists — from stars to thoughts — participates in a single energetic and informational matrix. Consciousness, in this context, ceases to be a mere byproduct of the brain and begins to appear as a *fundamental aspect of the very fabric of reality.*

It is precisely at this point that the dialogue between *quantum physics* and *psi phenomena* (telepathy, precognition, psychokinesis) becomes intellectually legitimate.

Dean Radin and other researchers propose that such phenomena are *spontaneous expressions of universal nonlocality,* manifesting through consciousness itself.

In his "pseudotelepathy game," Radin imagines how two observers — *Jack and Jill* — could, by sharing pairs of entangled particles, respond coherently to random questions without any communication.

The outcome would perfectly simulate *ideal telepathy.*

What was once deemed "impossible" under the classical worldview emerges, in the light of quantum mechanics, as a *natural consequence of the fundamental interconnection of the cosmos.*

If particles can remain correlated beyond space and time, why not *minds*, composed of the same energetic substrate? The hypothesis, though bold, remains coherent within a *nonlocal ontology.*

The question that inevitably follows is this:

If the universe has been entangled since its very beginning — and if consciousness is one of the expressions of that unified field — *where does one body end and another begin?*

The boundaries of the self, like those of matter, dissolve into a single field of information and presence.
The ancient Hermetic axiom regains its timeless validity: *"All is in all, and all is in one."*

"The universe is not made of things, but of relations."
— *Carlo Rovelli*

CHAPTER 5 — PSI IN THE LABORATORY

Telepathy, Clairvoyance, and Precognition

"Mind precedes matter; thought is the secret mold of form."
— *Hermes Trismegistus*

For more than a century, men and women of scientific spirit have sought, with rigor and persistence, to probe the invisible boundaries of the mind.
Their goal: to capture, under controlled conditions, the phenomena that appear to transcend the five senses.
Despite institutional resistance and the lingering prejudice of positivism, a growing body of empirical evidence — solid, replicable, and statistically irrefutable — has accumulated.
Today, the serious debate no longer concerns *whether* these phenomena exist, but *what* they are and *what they mean*.

Experiments in *Extra-Sensory Perception (ESP)* have evolved from curiosity to methodology.
From the earliest rudimentary tests to modern research in neurophysiology and applied statistics, *psi science* has passed through decades of experimental refinement, eliminating alternative explanations and expanding the

credibility of the impossible.

The First Experiments — Card Guessing and Telepathy

In the 1930s, J. B. Rhine at Duke University systematized the first rigorous tests of telepathy and clairvoyance using *Zener cards* — simple symbols designed to measure perception beyond chance.
In collaboration with Pratt and Pearce, Rhine conducted extensive series of experiments under absolute control and supervision.
The most striking result: *odds of 10^{27} to one* against chance — roughly a billion billion billion to one.
In practical terms, a statistical impossibility by conventional standards.

The Transmission of Drawings — Thought as Image

The American writer *Upton Sinclair*, in *Mental Radio*, reported remarkable experiments in which his wife, *Mary Craig Sinclair*, reproduced with striking accuracy drawings he visualized from a distance.
Shapes, symbols, and even emotional tone seemed to cross space as *mental waves*.
Independently, in France, *René Warcollier* published *Mind to Mind*, documenting telepathic drawing transmissions across continents.
Both observed consistent patterns in the way the mind translates images into symbolic impressions — suggesting a kind of *inner physics* of imagery and intention.

Remote Viewing — Transcending Space

In the 1970s, *SRI International (Stanford Research Institute)*

developed the *remote viewing* protocol, in which a "viewer" described distant or hidden locations without prior knowledge.
Series conducted by *Harold Puthoff* and *Russell Targ*, followed by experiments at the *PEAR Laboratory* (*Princeton Engineering Anomalies Research*), produced statistically significant results — with odds of millions to one against chance.
Observers, in states of light trance or focused attention, described geographic, architectural, and emotional details of unknown sites with astonishing precision.
Space, like time, appeared *malleable to consciousness.*

Meta-Analyses — The Weight of the Whole

When hundreds of independent studies are combined, the strength of the phenomenon becomes nearly overwhelming.

Psi in Dreams: At the *Maimonides Dream Laboratory* in New York, researchers tested whether telepathically sent images could influence dream content.
The meta-analysis of these experiments revealed hit rates so high that the odds of pure chance were estimated at *22 billion to one.*

Ganzfeld Experiments: In this method, participants are placed under mild sensory deprivation — a state between waking and dreaming.
An analysis of 88 studies revealed an average hit rate of *32%*, when chance would predict only *25%*.
The probability of this being random: *29 quintillion to one.*
By comparison, winning the lottery is far less likely.

The Sense of Being Watched: Even after rigorous

statistical corrections — including the *trim and fill* method to eliminate publication bias — results remained highly significant.
Final probability: *202 octodecillion to one* (a number followed by 59 zeros).
The body appears to *"know" when it is being observed,* even without any detectable sensory cues.

Unconscious Psi — The Body That Knows Before the Mind

Recent studies indicate that consciousness is not the only channel of psi perception.
Physiological reactions — such as *skin conductance, heart rate variability,* and *brain-wave patterns* — show anticipatory responses to stimuli not yet presented.
In double-blind experiments, the body reacts *seconds before* an emotional image appears on the screen.
It is as if the human organism, in its entirety, is connected to an informational field that transcends the linear sequence of time.

Experimental parapsychology thus reveals not mere anomalies, but a *silent revolution* in our understanding of mind.
The evidence suggests that *thought, emotion, and intention* are not confined to the brain but participate in a *living, intelligent network* that permeates reality itself.
The laboratory — once a symbol of skepticism — becomes the new *temple of the invisible.*

"The mind is the instrument through which the universe becomes aware of itself."
— *Sri Aurobindo*

CHAPTER 6 — MIND OVER MATTER

The Power of Intention

"Will is the primordial energy; the universe is its visible form."
— *Eliphas Lévi*

Among all psi phenomena, *psychokinesis* — or *psycho-kinesis* — occupies the most delicate and subversive territory in scientific inquiry.

It not only challenges the materialist paradigm but threatens the conceptual foundation of classical physics itself: the assumption that causality is one-way, and that mind is a product rather than a force.

Yet a century of disciplined research has revealed a consistent, subtle, and irreducible pattern: the mind appears, in some mysterious way, to interact with the physical world *nonlocally.*

From the earliest dice experiments of the early twentieth century, hints of mental influence on randomness were already evident.

Dean Radin, in a monumental meta-analysis of all studies published between 1935 and 1987, demonstrated an overall result equivalent to 10^{96} *to one* against chance —

a statistical magnitude that, in any other field, would be considered definitive proof.

With the advent of electronic technology, dice were replaced by *Random Number Generators (RNGs)* — devices based on genuinely unpredictable quantum processes.
In meticulously controlled experiments, participants attempted to *mentally "nudge"* the behavior of RNGs, producing slight deviations from the expected 50/50 distribution of zeros and ones.
The cumulative analysis — spanning over *490 independent studies* across multiple laboratories — revealed a robust statistical correlation between *intention and outcome.*
Small in magnitude, but consistent in direction.

The implication is profound: the human mind seems capable of subtly modulating the behavior of random physical systems.
But the phenomenon takes on a *philosophical dimension* when one observes that these deviations occur not only in individual experiments but also in *collective contexts.*

This realization gave rise to the *Global Consciousness Project* — a planetary network of RNGs distributed across dozens of countries.
These devices, connected in real time, record statistical fluctuations that appear to correlate with moments of intense collective emotion — such as the *September 11 attacks,* the *Indian Ocean tsunami,* or the *funeral of Princess Diana.*
During such events, the generators' randomness decreases significantly, as though the *mental field of humanity itself vibrates in unison,* resonating through the statistical fabric of reality.
This hypothesis of a *"field consciousness,"* or *global mind,*

suggests that consciousness is *not confined to the skull*, but participates in a living network of cosmic information.

Yet the central enigma remains: *how does this interaction occur?*

The traditional model — of the mind "pushing" particles — may be metaphorically useful but ontologically naïve.

Researchers such as *Helmut Schmidt* and *Edwin May* proposed alternative interpretations, among them the *Decision Augmentation Theory (DAT)*.

According to DAT, the effect of psychokinesis does not arise from a mental force acting upon matter, but from the mind's *unconscious precognition* selecting the optimal moment to act — aligning itself with futures already compatible with the desired intention.

In this view, *the mind does not move matter; it chooses the future.*

This reformulation shifts the question from *energy to information*, bringing psychokinesis closer to both *quantum physics* and the *mystical traditions* that have long viewed reality as an expression of consciousness.

In *spiritual alchemy* and *Hermeticism, will* — *Thelema* — is not seen as brute force but as an *ordering principle* operating through resonance and harmony.

Thus, the mind does not "violate" the laws of nature; it acts from a deeper level where *law and consciousness are one.*

From this perspective, psychokinesis is not merely an experimental curiosity but a glimpse into a *unified cosmology* in which intention, time, and matter are different manifestations of the same continuum.

To study the power of intention is, therefore, more than to measure statistics — it is to *probe the invisible link between thought and being, between the human and the divine.*

"Pure will, free from desire and self, is the channel through which Spirit shapes the world."
— *Sri Aurobindo*

PART III — MECHANISMS AND PRACTICES OF EXPANDED CONSCIOUSNESS

CHAPTER 7 — THE UNCONSCIOUS AS BRIDGE

Psychological Perspectives

Access to *psychic experience* seems not to reside in the conscious, analytical, and rational mind, but rather in the depths of the *unconscious* — where the boundaries of the self grow permeable and psychic reality mingles with the fabric of the world.

It is within this obscure yet fertile domain that anomalous connections arise, and the limits between the inner and the outer become fluid.

Various schools of psychology — from psychoanalysis to analytical psychology — have offered models to understand this region and its role as mediator between the individual mind and the larger field of reality, shedding light on possible mechanisms underlying *psi phenomena*.

Sigmund Freud, though publicly cautious, admitted in private writings his fascination with *telepathy.*

As noted by Matheus Augusto, Freud regarded it as an *archaic form of communication* — a vestige of the pre-verbal, symbiotic bond between mother and child, a language of *affect preceding speech.*

In certain clinical settings, he observed that such phenomena tended to appear in moments of intense emotional transference, suggesting that telepathy might be *modulated by unconscious affective bonds.*

Thus, the unconscious would not merely be a repository of repressed drives, but also a *subtle channel of psychic interconnection.*

Carl Gustav Jung expanded this vision through his notion of the *collective unconscious* — a transpersonal substratum containing *archetypes*, primordial forms of experience and meaning.

For Jung, these patterns not only shape the contents of the mind but also organize the phenomenal world itself, functioning as *formal principles* that give coherence to synchronistic events.

He saw the unconscious as a *living matrix*, a "common sea" in which the individual psyche is immersed and, in certain states, recognizes itself as part of a greater whole.

Contemporary psychology, in dialogue with parapsychological research, offers findings consistent with these ideas.

Studies cited by *Dean Radin* indicate that individuals prone to psychic experiences tend to share certain traits: *openness to experience, high absorptiveness,* and *low latent inhibition.*

The latter — the tendency not to filter stimuli considered irrelevant — can predispose one to either *psychosis or creative genius.*

Paradoxically, it is precisely this *cognitive permeability* that seems to allow subtle, symbolic, and unconscious information to cross into waking awareness.

Much like mystics who learn to silence the noise of the

mind to hear the *"breath of the Spirit,"* the individual with low latent inhibition lives more exposed to the *field of resonance between the psychic and the cosmic.*

They perceive the invisible through the cracks of the visible.

In Jungian terms, such a person is one whose *bridge between the ego and the Self* remains partially open.

If the unconscious is indeed the *intermediate matrix* between the human and the trans-human, between the personal and the universal, then cultivating states that access it — through *meditation, art, dreams, or symbolic contemplation* — is not merely an inner exercise.

It is a *method of expanding consciousness itself* beyond the habitual frontiers of the mind.

CHAPTER 8 — THE DISCIPLINE OF MIND AND SPIRIT

Practical Paths to Transcendence

Throughout the centuries, diverse spiritual and esoteric traditions have forged *systematic methods* for disciplining the mind, strengthening the will, and opening the channels of subtle perception.

These practices are not random techniques but are grounded in cohesive *cosmological visions* concerning the nature of consciousness and its intimate relationship with the cosmos.

This chapter offers a practical guide, distilled from the wisdom of *Franz Bardon* and *Khawaja Shamsuddin Azeemi*, for those who aspire to begin their own inner development — emphasizing *patience, perseverance,* and *self-discipline* as the fundamental pillars of this ascending journey.

Foundations of Magical Training (According to Franz Bardon)

The basis of any authentic spiritual development lies in *rigorous self-knowledge,* for as the ancient oracle declared:

"Know thyself, and thou shalt know the universe and the gods."

• Self-Analysis and the Magical Diary

The first step on this path is *unsparing self-examination.*

The aspirant must keep a diary in which to record both imperfections and virtues, classifying each trait according to the four primordial elements (*Fire, Air, Water, Earth*).

This act of conscious self-observation forms the most essential preliminary work for achieving the *magical equilibrium* required for further development.

• Concentration of Thought

The next stage is *mastery of the mind* — that most powerful yet treacherous of instruments.

Bardon prescribes a sequence of progressive exercises: concentration on a single thought, then upon an object, visual images, sounds, and emotions.

The goal is to maintain uninterrupted focus for at least five minutes, laying the foundation for the mind to become a *precise instrument of the spirit.*

Breath and Meditation Practices (Combining Azeemi and Bardon)

Breath is the *sacred bridge* between body and mind — the conduit through which the system is charged with the *vital energy* permeating all things.

• Breathing Exercises (Pranayama)

Khawaja Azeemi outlines detailed exercises to strengthen the nerves and awaken latent faculties within every human being.

The "Eighth Exercise," for instance, involves alternating and timed respiration: close the right nostril with the right

thumb and inhale through the left for ten seconds.
Then close both nostrils, retaining the breath for forty-five seconds.
Next, release the thumb and exhale through the right nostril for ten seconds.
Repeat the cycle in reverse — inhaling through the right and exhaling through the left.
This practice *harmonizes the polarities* within the practitioner.

• **Muraqbah (Contemplative Meditation)**
This Sufi exercise aims to focus the mind and expand awareness beyond conventional limits.
One example is to visualize a radiant point of light at the navel or the heart, imagining its rays expanding outward and being absorbed by the entire universe — recognizing thereby the *fundamental unity* between *microcosm and macrocosm*.

Visualization and Projection Techniques

Once concentration is achieved, the student may begin to *project consciousness and energy actively,* transcending the boundaries of ordinary perception.

• **Crystal and Mirror Gazing**
As described by *Swami Panchadasi,* the use of a crystal or mirror is not for gazing *into* the object, but for using it as a point of focus that stills the conscious mind and allows *astral vision* to rise from the depths of being.
It is through the *silence of the surface* that the depths reveal their secrets.

• **Elemental Projection**
An advanced Bardonian exercise involves drawing one of

the elements — for instance, *Fire* with its quality of heat — into the body through breath and imagination, containing it, and then projecting it outward into the environment. With practice, this projection can become so tangible as to be *perceptible to others,* demonstrating the concrete reality of subtle forces.

Suggested Practice Schedule

Consistency is more important than intensity.
A brief but *daily routine* is essential for lasting spiritual progress.

Practice	Suggested Frequency	Duration	Focus
Self-Analysis Diary	Daily (morning & night)	5–10 min	Self-observation and elemental balance
Concentration Exercise	Daily	5–10 min	Focus on a single point, image, or sound
Breathing Exercise	Daily (morning and/or night)	15–20 cycles	Strengthening the nervous system and vitality
Muraqbah / Meditation	Daily (after breathing)	15–20 min	Inner focus and expansion of consciousne

Visualization / Projection	Weekly	20–30 min	Development of astral sight and energy control

Warning

Both *Azeemi* and *Bardon* emphasize that these disciplines require *patience and perseverance.*
Spiritual advancement is measured in *years, not days.*
As in all sacred arts, development should ideally be supervised by an *experienced guide* who has already walked the path and can illuminate its darker passages.

If the *disciplines of mind* are the *engine* of expanded consciousness, then the *condition of the physical body* is its *vehicle.*

The way we tune our biological instrument plays a crucial role in this transformative process, for it is through the *harmony of body, mind, and spirit* that true magic manifests within human existence.

CHAPTER 9 — THE BODY AS ANTENNA

*Subtle Physiology and the
Web of Vital Energy*

In the depths of the esoteric traditions, the physical body is not conceived as a mere biological machine, but as a *living, finely tuned instrument* — an *antenna* designed to receive, process, and transmit the energetic currents that permeate the cosmos.

Establishing a dialogue between *mental practice* and a deeper understanding of *subtle physiology* proves essential, for physical factors function as true *master keys* capable of either unblocking or sealing the channels of psychic development.

The Alchemy of Nutrition and the Portals of Perception

One of the most direct and powerful tools for such fine-tuning lies in *diet*.

Khawaja Shamsuddin Azeemi, in his investigations, recounts studies by "spiritual scientists" who discovered a profound correspondence:

sugar and sweet substances act as builders of the *conscious senses* that anchor us to the material world, whereas *salt* activates the *unconscious senses* — the gateways to the metaphysical realm.

Azeemi himself described a period of *nine months of total abstinence from sugar,* culminating in the spontaneous development of faculties such as *remote viewing* and *telepathy.*

Yet he adds an essential caution, echoing ancient wisdom: no one should alter diet drastically or restrict salt or sugar intake without the explicit guidance of a qualified master. *The manipulation of these forces requires both knowledge and reverence.*

The Hidden Anatomy: Polarities and Vital Fluids

Franz Bardon deepens this view with his masterful *"occult anatomy,"* unveiling the body not as a homogeneous unit but as a dynamic system of *polarities in constant interaction.* He postulated the existence of two fundamental fluids:

- **Electric Fluid** — associated with *Fire,* expressing active, expansive, centrifugal force.
- **Magnetic Fluid** — associated with *Water,* expressing passive, contractive, centripetal force.

Every region of the body possesses a specific polarity — an *energetic map* the magician must learn to master in order to govern his own microcosmic organism.

This subtle architecture may be outlined as follows:

Body Part	Polarity	Description (Bardon)
Head	Right: Electric / Left: Magnetic /	The right hemisphere channels active, projective force; the left attracts

Eyes	Interior: Magnetic	and assimilates; the core functions as a receptive vortex.
	Right: Electric / Left: Electric / Interior: Magnetic	The outer vision projects will; the inner depth (retina, optic nerve) is receptive.
Hands	Right: Magnetic / Left: Electric / Interior: Neutral	The right hand attracts and condenses; the left projects and emits; the center of the palm is a point of balance and transmutation.
Fingers (Right Hand)	Sides: Electric / Core: Neutral	Emit electrical force laterally; the inner structure channels pure flow.
Fingers (Left Hand)	Both sides: Electric / Core: Neutral	Emit dual electrical force; the remainder maintains neutrality.

Vital Energy: Accumulation, Impregnation, and the Law of Biomagnetism

Beyond the polarity map, Bardon teaches the nature and manipulation of *vital energy* (*Od, Prana, Chi*).
Through precise breathing and concentration exercises, this primordial force can be *accumulated within the body.*
Its power, however, lies in a higher faculty: the ability to be *impregnated* with a *desire, intention,* or *thought-form.*

Here the *Law of Biomagnetism* comes into play:
vital energy not only carries conceptual quality but can be

programmed with coordinates of *time and space.*

Thus, the adept — mastering this art — may project charged energy to manifest its effect at a specific location in the macrocosm and at a chosen future moment.

It is the *materialization of will through the etheric substance.*

From the Biological Antenna to the Technological Symphony: The Future of Consciousness

While the ancients focused on refining the biological body into an ever more sensitive *antenna for the harmonies of the universe,* modern technology now unveils unprecedented horizons.

It offers the possibility of extending and interconnecting the human mind in ways once confined to the realm of *myth and prophecy.*

We stand, therefore, on the threshold of a new frontier: the exploration of the *future of consciousness itself* — where the knowledge of subtle physiology and the tools of technology may converge in a *cosmic symphony,* redefining the limits of being and perception.

The body remains the *fundamental temple* — yet now, potentially, connected to a *quantum web of information and energy* that transcends the individual, pointing toward a deeper realization of the Hermetic axiom:

"As above, so below; as within, so without."

PART IV — THE FUTURE OF CONSCIOUSNESS: NEUROTECHNOLOGY, ETHICS, AND THE GREAT EVOLUTIONARY SYMPHONY

CHAPTER 10 — THE CONNECTED BRAIN

Brain–Machine Interfaces and the Awakening of the Global Mind

The millennial quest for *telepathy* — that silent communion of minds cultivated by mystical traditions as the crown of inner development — now finds its emerging technological mirror.
Science, in its ascending trajectory, is beginning to *create externally what the initiates sought to awaken within.*
This convergence is no mere historical coincidence but a sign of the times: a deep resonance between the *arcane and the technological*, dissolving the borders between the "psychic" and the "digital," and revealing both as expressions of a single, primordial impulse — the transcendence of individual consciousness.

Neurotechnologies and the Dawn of Synthetic Telepathy

Neurotechnologies — defined as any artifact that interacts with or deciphers the mysteries of the brain — are advancing at an exponential rate.

At the heart of this revolution stand the *Brain–Computer Interfaces* (BCIs).

Pioneering companies now openly declare their purpose: to develop *neural implants* that allow users to control digital systems through *pure thought*.

This is not telepathy in the classical sense, but a *synthetic telepathy* — a bridge of silicon and neurons, materializing the ancient dream of direct mind-to-mind communication.

Visions of the Connected Future: From Enhancement to Collective Symphony

Two main trajectories emerge on this horizon:

1. The Path of Individual Enhancement

This approach focuses on optimizing human capacities through direct integration with digital systems — expanding memory, accelerating cognition, and creating neuro-motor control channels.

Its goal: the improvement of the individual *within* the existing paradigm.

2. Miguel Nicolelis's Radical Vision — The "Brainet"

The Brazilian neuroscientist proposes a quantum leap: not connecting a single brain to a machine, but *many brains to each other* — forming what he calls a *Brainet*, a *distributed organic computer*.

In this architecture, multiple human brains synchronize their neural patterns to operate as a *single cognitive entity* — sharing information, solving complex problems, and generating insights beyond the reach of any isolated mind.

It is the *technological materialization of the mystical idea of collective consciousness*.

The Subtle Echo: Field Consciousness and the Implicit Global Mind

Curiously, Nicolelis's vision of an interconnected mind finds a deep echo in *field consciousness* research.

The *Global Consciousness Project* (GCP), led by Dean Radin, operates a worldwide network of *Random Number Generators* (RNGs).

These devices, designed to produce truly random sequences, consistently show *statistically significant deviations from randomness* during moments of global emotional coherence — catastrophes, mass celebrations, collective grief.

Such fluctuations suggest that a subtle but measurable form of *global mind* may already exist — a *resonance within the quantum fabric of reality*, uniting human consciousness at an implicit level.

Technology, therefore, does not *create* this connection from nothing — it *reveals, digitizes, and amplifies* it.

BCIs and Brainets thus appear as instruments for manifesting, on the physical plane, a unity that already pulses — silent and unseen — in the subtle realm.

Synthetic vs. Mystical Telepathy: A Mirror Comparison

Aspect	Synthetic Telepathy (BCI / Brainet)	Mystical Telepathy (Inner Development)
Nature	Digital-neural interface based on electrochemical	Subtle resonance between energetic and mental fields.

Mechanism	Decoding and transmitting neural patterns. signals.	Vibrational attunement and perception beyond the senses.
Scope	Limited by technology and infrastructure.	Theoretically boundless, transcending space and time.
Dependency	Requires external hardware and energy.	Emerges from inner spiritual development.
State of Consciousness	Possible in ordinary waking states.	Typically associated with deep meditative or ecstatic states.

The Ethical Threshold: The Abysses and Promises of the Interconnected Mind

As we approach a future where thoughts can be read, emotions decoded, and minds linked through technology, we face ethical abysses of unprecedented depth:

• **The Sanctity of the Self:**
Who will have access to our most intimate thoughts?
How do we protect the last frontier of privacy — the *inner sanctuary of the mind*?
The prospect of *neural hacking* or *digital subliminal manipulation* poses an existential threat to individual autonomy.

• **The Redefinition of Identity:**

If multiple brains operate as a Brainet, where does the "I" reside?
Does individuality dissolve into the collective?
How can we preserve the *singularity of the soul* amid the neural symphony?

- **Equity of Access:**
Who will benefit from these mind-amplifying technologies?
Will humanity be divided between the "connected" and the "disconnected," the "enhanced" and the "natural"?

- **Collective Responsibility:**
If a Brainet commits an error or causes harm, *who* is accountable?
A collective mind dissolves the traditional notion of individual responsibility.

Technology is not neutral — it is a *mirror that amplifies our collective choices.*
In creating interfaces for the mind, we are not merely building tools; we are *redesigning the foundations of human experience.*
The great ethical challenge, therefore, is not only to regulate technology but to *evolve our wisdom* — to use these powers not to dominate, but to harmonize; not to fragment, but to unite; not to replace the mystery of consciousness, but to *celebrate and expand it* toward a deeper understanding of who we are — and who we may yet become — as a *single, interconnected humanity*, woven both by the threads of technology and by the invisible fibers of spirit.

"The future of consciousness will not be determined by our neurotechnological advances,
but by our ability to respond to them with integrity,

compassion, and cosmic vision."

CHAPTER 11 — THE ETHICS OF THE OPEN MIND

Privacy, Enhancement, and the Sacred Duty of Responsibility

The power to *decode the archetypes of thought* and *influence the labyrinths of consciousness* — whether through psychic faculties forged in meditative silence or through neurotechnologies unveiling the brain's architecture — carries within itself a responsibility of *cosmic proportion*.
As we lift the veil over the mysteries of the mind, we enter an *unprecedented ethical frontier*, demanding profound reflection on the pillars of privacy, the nature of identity, and the ultimate purpose of the power now unfolding in our hands.

The Profaned Sanctuary: The Crisis of Neuroprivacy

The most urgent question stands as guardian at the gate of this new world: *mental privacy*.
As the seminal document **"Neurotechnology"** warns, the capacity to decode another's unconscious brain activity

represents an unprecedented threat to autonomy — the *ultimate violation of the inner sanctum.*

In response, thinkers such as *Marcello Ienca* and *Roberto Adorno* have raised a conceptual beacon: the need for a **"right to mental privacy."**

This neuro-specific protection must stand as an *inviolable shield* against the unauthorized collection, storage, and analysis of neural data — the very essence of the self.

Redesigning the Human Condition: Enhancement and the Abyss of Equity

The debate extends to the horizon of *human enhancement.*

Transhumanism, in its aspiration to transcend biological limits, provokes questions that strike the core of distributive justice:

if cognitive enhancement becomes reality, *who will have access to this new source of power?*

How can we reconcile individual striving with the imperative of the common good?

Neuroethics forces us to confront the fundamental enigma: *what does it truly mean to be human?*

And what boundaries — if any — should we draw in our own transformative journey?

The Arcane Echo: Ancient Warnings and the Perils of Power

These technological dilemmas find a prophetic echo in the ancient esoteric warnings.

Masters such as *Swami Panchadasi* and *Franz Bardon* vehemently cautioned against the selfish use of mental influence.

Panchadasi denounced the "low-grade occult teachers"

who instructed disciples to manipulate souls for material gain — a vile perversion of true knowledge, which should *elevate, not enslave.*

Bardon, in turn, established an unbreakable law: *the ennoblement of character must advance in step with the development of power.*

The pursuit of power for its own sake, he warned, is a seed that inevitably bears the fruits of stagnation or ruin.

Technological Ethics vs. Esoteric Ethics: Two Paths, One Challenge

Ethical Dimension	Neurotechnology	Esoteric Traditions
Core Danger	Neural data violation; algorithmic manipulation.	Energetic manipulation; ego-driven mental domination.
Proposed Safeguard	Right to neuroprivacy; technical regulation.	Moral purification; prior spiritual discipline.
Greatest Risk	Loss of autonomy; technological inequality.	Spiritual stagnation; karmic downfall.
Governing Principle	Distributive justice; informed consent.	Elemental balance; harmony with universal law.
Ultimate Goal	Preserve human dignity in the digital age.	Achieve divine unity through service and love.

Wisdom as Compass: The Final Call

Whether through the *silicon–neuron interface* or through the discipline that attunes the subtle centers, *power over consciousness* requires, as a **sine qua non condition**, the cultivation of *wisdom*.

As contemporary neuroethicists conclude,

"Now more than ever, science, technoscience, and all forms of technology must return to the reflective cultivation of human wisdom."

This wisdom is not mere accumulation of knowledge but the *deep perception* that our power grows in *direct proportion to our responsibility*.

We stand on the threshold of an era where the mind can be read, linked, and even rewritten.

In such a moment, *ethics is not a brake but a beacon* — the light by which we must steer our course.

True enhancement — whether technological or spiritual — lies not in the *expansion of capacities* but in the *expansion of compassion, integrity, and awareness* that in the vast ocean of consciousness, *we are all one*.

Power without wisdom is a lightning bolt without direction; wisdom without power is a lamp hidden beneath a basket.

Our sacred task is to unite them — and in that union, rediscover the divine purpose of existence.

FINAL CONSIDERATIONS: TOWARD UNITY WITH KNOWLEDGE

The Symphony of Knowledge

We have traversed an archetypal journey, beginning in the veiled mysteries of ancient oracles and the complex hermetic models that mapped the cosmos as a living fabric of correspondences. We journeyed through the laboratories of parapsychology, where the "impossible" revealed itself as statistically undeniable, and the realms of quantum physics, where paradox became the language of reality. We plunged into the depths of the unconscious —that primordial ocean where archetypes and the seeds of human potential reside—and explored practical disciplines for its development, culminating at the dizzying frontiers of neurotechnology and the ethical abysses unfolding on the horizon of the future.

The Central Thesis: Consciousness as Cosmic Ocean

Throughout this journey, a central thesis emerged from the shadows, strengthening like an inextinguishable

THE HIDDEN REALITY OF MIND

light: consciousness is not an isolated phenomenon, a mere biochemical accident confined within the fortress of the skull. On the contrary, converging evidence from seemingly disparate fields—from mysticism to science, from philosophy to experimentation—suggests that consciousness is a fundamental facet, an essential expression of a deeply intertwined and intrinsically meaningful reality.

The visionary metaphor of philosopher William James, cited by Dean Radin, captures this truth with poetic precision: our individual consciousnesses are like "islands in the sea," apparently separate on the turbulent surface of manifestation. Yet "all islands are connected beneath the ocean," merging into a "continuum of cosmic consciousness"—the common reservoir, the inexhaustible source from which we all emerge and to which we all return. This is the great secret both veiled and revealed: separation is an illusion of perspective; unity, the underlying reality.

The Next Revolution: The Fusion of Knowledge

The next great revolution in human understanding will not spring from a single field of knowledge, however revolutionary it may be. It will arise from the harmonious integration between objective science—with its rigorous method and its quest for universal laws—and subjective, contemplative wisdom—with its profound immersion in direct experience and intuitive understanding of ultimate truths. The future of knowledge lies in this sacred fusion: the external investigation of the universe (the cosmos) in dialogue with the internal exploration of consciousness (the psyche).

The ultimate goal of this quest, whether expressed in the

symbolic language of magic, the theology of religion, or the dialectic of philosophy, is always the same: unification. It is Franz Bardon's "unity with God"—the realization of the microcosm as a mirror of the macrocosm. It is the Socratic ideal, inscribed at the portal of the Temple of Delphi: "Know thyself" in order to then "know the universe and the gods." It is the understanding, through gnosis—through direct and lived knowledge—that we are integral parts of a greater whole, inseparable threads in the cosmic tapestry of Being.

The Limitless Horizon: Beyond the Frontiers of Belief

In this incessant quest for the unity of knowledge, perhaps there are no definitive limits to what we can discover, both about the vastness of the cosmos and about the abyssal depths of our own inner being. As echoed by philosopher Willis Harman, in a phrase that resonates like an oracle for our age:

"Perhaps the only limits of the human mind are those we believe in."

This statement is not an invitation to delusion, but a call to courage. Courage to question the dogmas of materialist science, courage to explore the territories of mystical experience without prejudice, courage to integrate knowledge and glimpse a reality broader, more complex, and more marvelous than any current model can conceive.

Thus, we conclude our journey not with final answers, but with an open invitation. The path toward unity with knowledge is an endless way, a pilgrimage of consciousness toward its own source. May each step taken in this direction—whether through a quantum experiment, a deep meditation, an ethical reflection, or the responsible use of technology—bring us closer to this supreme realization: that in the silence between thoughts and in the space between particles, we already are, and have always been, One with the Knowledge that is Life itself.

BIBLIOGRAPHY

AZEEMI, Khawaja Shamsuddin. Learn Telepathy. [s.l.]: [s.n.], [s.d.].

AUGUSTO, Matheus. The Unconscious and Telepathy: a dialogue between Psychoanalysis and Occultism. [s.d.]. Available at: Lume UFRGS.

BARDON, Franz. Practical Magic: The Path of the Adept. [s.l.]: [s.n.], [s.d.].

JUNG, C.G. Synchronicity: a principle of acausal connections. IJUSC, [s.d.].

MARQUES, Stella Maris Souza. Anomalistic Psychology and Epistemology: The Challenges of Psychic Research in Psychology. [s.d.]. Available at: Institutional Repository - Federal University of Uberlândia.

OLIVEIRA, Nythamar de et al. Neurotechnology and Philosophy of Neuroscience. [s.l.]: [s.n.], [s.d.].

PANCHADASI, Swami. Telepathy, Mind Reading, Clairvoyance, and Other Psychic Powers. [s.l.]: [s.n.], [s.d.].

RADIN, Dean. Entangled Minds: Scientific evidence of telepathy, clairvoyance and other psychic phenomena. São Paulo: Aleph, [s.d.].

REICHOW, J. R. C.; PARRA, A. Mind-Matter Interaction Within the Perspective of Anomalistic Psychology: A Review of Research Conducted in the Last Five Years. [s.d.].

Available at: Pepsic.

Printed in Dunstable, United Kingdom